NEVER FEAR,
NEVER QUIT

NEVER FEAR, NEVER QUIT

A STORY OF COURAGE AND PERSEVERANCE

JOE TYE

Delacorte **Press**

Published by
Delacorte Press
Bantam Doubleday Dell Publishing Group, Inc.
1540 Broadway
New York, New York 10036

Library of Congress Cataloging in Publication Data

Tye, Joe.
    Never fear, never quit : a story of courage and perseverance /
by Joe Tye.
        p.   cm.
    ISBN 0-385-31836-7
    1. Courage.   2. Perseverance (Ethics)   I. Title.
BJ1533.C8T94   1997
179'.6—dc20   96-34124
                                                                    CIP

This book was previously published in
a slightly different version by Paradox 21 Press.

Manufactured in the United States of America
Published simultaneously in Canada

May 1997

10 9 8 7 6 5 4 3 2 1

BVG

Dedicated to C. Everett Koop, M.D.,
and to the memory of Ann Moore, Dr. P.H.,
who, through their examples, show that to create
constructive change you must
Never Fear and *Never Quit*

CONTENTS

Note to the Reader

This is a true story.

"You mean some guy named Paul Peterson really jumped off a cliff and was saved by this strange miracle worker named Rafe, who then helped him learn to overcome fear, doubt, and adversity?" you might ask.

Well, I would reply, the story is true in that it has integrity, a wholeness that we can each recognize in our own life's experience. It's not just *a* story, it's a part of *The Story* that's played itself out millions of times before Paul met Rafe on that cliff top, and many times since. Perhaps in your life. I know it has in mine.

Rafe is faith. Faith that there is meaning in all life, including your own. That no one who is trying to do what is right will be allowed to labor unaided. Faith that although adversity may at first seem to weaken and hurt you, it will eventually strengthen and heal you. That when you are ready to learn, teachers will appear. That in the darkest moment the light is not long in coming.

Rafe *will* be there when you hit bottom, and you'll know you've hit bottom when Rafe appears. You'll know it's Rafe by this: The serendipity is too amazing to believe it's a coincidence. Something is about to happen that was meant to be, something that is truly miraculous.

Miracle is not too strong a word for the connections that faith will make, for the changes that are possible in your life, but you must first understand what a miracle is, and what it is not.

A miracle is not a magic trick. It is the bringing about of a change that would previously have been thought impossible.

A miracle is not an event. It is a process.

A miracle is not a gift. It is something earned through hard work and painful introspection.

A miracle is not free. It comes with strings attached, and if you're not willing to share it, you will be unable to keep it.

In truth the greatest miracle is this: the miracle of profound self-transformation. Many of the miracles recorded in history are simply metaphors for this simple truth, that we each have the power in our own hands to create the miracle of becoming the person we were meant to be.

The twenty principles of courage and perseverance that serve as chapter headings for this book aren't mine; they come from a universal and timeless wisdom. Others taught them to me. I hope that they can transform your life as they have mine.

NEVER FEAR

1

CARING IS THE ROOT OF COURAGE

WHEN THE SUN TOUCHED THE WESTERN HORIZON, PAUSED, then slowly started back up into the sky, Paul Peterson knew it was going to be a long day.

It had already been a long day. Paul had been standing at cliff's edge for nearly an hour, watching the sun finish its daily arc and listening to the surf smash against the rocks below. This sunset would end a decade. Ten years of struggling to build his school, a safe place where sad-faced kids could find refuge from a faceless system. On this tenth anniversary of the Shay's Point School, that dream had been ended by the slash of a banker's eighty-dollar pen.

Ten years ago it had just been Paul himself, fresh out of law school and determined to save young people from being crushed by the penal system for committing crimes they hardly comprehended to be criminal. Now it was him and the family, the mortgages, the school, the ever-increasing critics, and the fewer-and-farther-between backers.

This morning he had cared. For the three-thousand-six-hundred-fiftieth day, he dragged himself out of bed after too little sleep, armored himself in a coat and tie, and set out for the fight. And lost. Everything.

Including the capacity to care.

Now he was leaning into a stiff shoreward breeze, waiting for the sun to disappear. Then he would take his last step.

"It's a beautiful evening for flying, isn't it?"

Paul started at the voice, which crept up from behind and slapped him on the back. Losing his balance, he twisted his body sideways, arms spinning frantically like the impotent rotors of a crippled helicopter.

As his feet left the ground, Paul felt the sensation of floating, momentarily suspended in motionless time. His eyes locked onto the faint pinprick of a star trying to burn its way into the darkening evening sky as he toppled back and began to accelerate earthward. Then, much too soon, he hit the ground.

After an agonizing moment of dark stillness, Paul drew what seemed an awfully lot like a living breath and opened his eyes to see the same star fighting for its spot in the twilight. There had been no tunnel of light, no flashing autobiography, no celestial choir or old friends at the gate. Just a quick fall, a sudden hard thump, and the dawning realization of pain. Real, human pain.

"Are you okay?"

It was the same voice, deep and rich. Paul looked to his side and saw a man of about his own age kneeling beside him. Long brown hair, thinning on the top, fluttered like prairie grass in a summer breeze. His dark, weathered skin

FEAR IS THE PARENT OF BOTH

COURAGE AND OF COWARDICE.

WHICH CHILD WILL YOU

CHOOSE TO RAISE?

suggested a life on the fishing boats. He wore the compassionate, bemused smile of a father trying not to laugh as he helped his child up from a spectacular tricycle wipeout.

"Here, let me give you a hand." The man pulled Paul to his feet without apparent effort and brushed off the back of his coat. They were standing fifty feet back from the edge of the cliff. At the spot where Paul had been standing was a tall, slender man with a brown trench coat just like his. He was watching the sun, now several degrees off the horizon. And rising.

A pair of sea gulls streaked by, flying tail-first and emitting a bizarre squawk. Paul closed his eyes and struggled to dredge up a memory of falling, of being broken on the rocks. Nothing short of being dead could explain this craziness.

"No, Paul, you didn't jump. At least not yet. Earthly time is moving in reverse. You might say that the drama that played itself out today is being un-acted."

The sun was huge above the horizon, dwarfing the man on the cliff. A jet airplane moved backward across the sky, erasing the brilliant white contrail that a moment ago had punctuated the orange firmament. Paul saw the man in the trench coat watch the sun edge its way higher into the sky, igniting the furrowed clouds as if the world's entire supply of fireworks had been requisitioned for this occasion. The figure dropped awkwardly to his knees and remained for a moment with his face in his hands, then just as awkwardly rose and started walking backward away from the cliff.

The fisherman put a hand on Paul's shoulder and guided him toward the path. They followed the figure in Paul's trench coat as he trudged backward down the hill, hands in pockets, eyes to the ground. At the parking lot they watched the figure unclose the car door, and stand there for a long while looking up the hill. He looked just like Paul—tall and thin, clean shaven, brown hair just a little too long for someone otherwise dressed like a middle-aged yuppie.

"You've had a bad day, my friend, and you're about to live it again—twice, I'm afraid." The fisherman smiled, not looking at all afraid. "And what's more, you're going to watch yourself do it. Come on, climb in."

The fisherman stepped through the back door of Paul's Chevy without even opening it, and motioned for Paul to follow. The trench-coated figure was backing his way into the driver's seat. "Hurry up," the fisherman shouted, "it's a lot harder to go through doors when the car is moving."

Paul stood frozen as he listened to the oddly distorted but unmistakable backfire of his old Chevy as the engine cut out. But the engine hadn't cut out. It was now idling roughly and sucking white puffs of smoke back into the tailpipe. The fisherman reached out from the car and yanked Paul through the closed rear door. He didn't feel a thing.

The other Paul—Paul could see now beyond a doubt that he was watching himself—put the car in drive and started backing out of the parking lot, eyes straight ahead.

"Hey! Watch where you're going, dummy, you're going to hit something!"

"He can't hear you," the fisherman said, "or see you. In fact only one of you is really real. By the way, why do you so often call yourself dummy?" He looked serious, as though he really expected an answer. Paul just snorted and looked out the window as the car accelerated backward away from the parking lot.

The car was out on Fontanella Avenue backing down the road at forty-five miles per hour. Looking out the side window, Paul saw a big golden retriever leap backward into the air and spit a tennis ball out of its mouth; the ball instantly reversed course, hit the ground just in front of the dog's feet as it landed on its hind legs, and then bounded back over its head into the hands of the young woman in the front yard. The dog raced backward and sat expectantly at her feet as she rubbed its head and put the ball back in her pocket. Paul vaguely remembered having seen this scene played out in a forward direction on the drive toward the cliffs.

"This is going to take all day if we don't speed things up," the fisherman said as he pulled a pocket watch out and wound it. The world began to whiz by as if in time-lapse photography, except that it was all whizzing by in reverse. The car raced backward down the exit ramp onto the interstate, with Paul wincing as the other "him" accelerated to seventy miles per hour without looking back. Just as quickly they were back on Main Street, flitting tail-first through city traffic.

"You look bewildered, my friend." Again that ancient, majestic voice. Paul almost expected to look over and see a statue of Moses, but it was still the fisherman with the infinite eyes. And that smile—was it heartrending sadness or bottomless joy? The man placed a hand on Paul's shoulder, firm and reassuring.

"My name is Rafe. You're taking this pretty well, but I imagine you'd like to know what's going on." The car was spiraling backward up the exit ramp of the First National Bank parking deck.

Paul nodded, so the man began. "How can I best explain it, this moving backward in time? Ordinary people see time the way a railroad engineer sees tracks—you pass over the cross ties one at a time: the ones behind you receding back into the distance, the ones up front always out of sight.

"When you enter a tunnel, you have no way of knowing when you will reach the light at the other side, you can only have faith that the tunnel won't go on forever.

"But I see time the way an eagle sees the railroad looking down from the air. All at once I can see the tracks behind and the tracks ahead. Depending upon my own airspeed or direction, the train below can be moving forward, backward, or standing still relative to my own position. Like this . . ."

The car had backed into a stall—Paul remembered parking in a handicapped space this morning because he was running late for an important meeting—when suddenly everything froze in place. The other Paul had a furious scowl on his face, and his clenched fist hovered about six inches above the dashboard. Paul rubbed the side of his hand, remembering the blow. Rafe clicked his pocket watch again, and the fist slammed off the dashboard as Paul's image stepped back out of the car, jammed the parking ticket under the windshield wiper, and banged his briefcase off the car hood.

They followed Paul's image as he paced backward toward the elevators. "When a train goes into a tunnel," Rafe continued, "the passengers may feel that they have been swallowed up by perpetual darkness, but from my

IF YOU LOSE HOPE,
YOU'RE JUST NOT LOOKING
FAR ENOUGH AHEAD.

vantage point in the sky I can see just how long they will be in there, and what awaits them on the other side."

As the other Paul pushed his way backward through the crowded bank lobby, people behind him glared angrily at his back, then looked shocked as the backs of their shoulders swung around to collide with the front of his, and then resumed their unsuspecting small talk as he steamed back toward the fateful conference room.

In the baroque elegance of the conference room Paul couldn't help but laugh at the bank's chief loan officer gesticulating madly while sounding like Alvin the Chipmunk speaking Russian. Two armed security guards walked backward into the room, looking over their shoulders as they entered. They turned slowly and stood at attention for a while as though just looking for an excuse to manhandle Paul's image, then raced backward out of the room with alarmed expressions and hands on their gun holsters.

Papers spilled out of briefcases and across the polished table—papers that Paul knew would destroy ten years of hard work and sacrifice. The papers then spilled back into the briefcases, and Paul's image walked backward out of the conference room. He didn't look angry now, he looked scared to death. They followed him back to the car.

The sun was high overhead as they backed through the gate, and Paul's image handed the ticket to the parking-ramp attendant. Familiar landmarks flashed by as they drove toward Paul's dream: the Shay's Point Alternative School. A decade ago it had been a rundown warehouse. For ten years Paul and Joan had sunk every hour, every dollar, into building this school for troubled young people as an alternative to reform school or prison.

It was a fight from the beginning. Some critics wanted the school closed because the students were made to follow strict rules and wear uniforms. Others wanted it closed because rewarding lawbreakers by putting them in a special school wasn't their idea of justice. And now all their wishes were about to come true. In about an hour, or an hour ago with time flowing backward, the bank would shut him down for failing to keep up on his loan payments.

"He looks awfully lonely, doesn't he?" Rafe watched Paul's image at his desk punching away on a calculator and unscribbling notes from financial reports.

"Lonely and frightened—somehow the two always seem to go together."

Paul's image stuffed his papers back into the briefcase and retreated through the building toward the parking lot, nodding curtly at uniformed youngsters as they scurried backward through the corridors. The dashboard clock was counting its way back toward eight o'clock by the time they shot down the exit ramp onto the freeway toward the suburbs. Paul noticed a growing coffee aroma, and realized that his image was gradually undrinking the cup on the dashboard.

The car slowed and came to a stop just past the driveway of his white Victorian home. No matter which way time was flowing, Joan's landscaping was beautiful.

The driver gazed at the house for a moment, put the car in reverse and, oblivious to the passengers in the backseat, twisted his neck to see the road behind while he pulled forward into the driveway. They followed him as he backed his way up the walk, said good-bye to the children, kissed his wife at the front door, and then backed into the kitchen.

"Even this morning, I knew." Paul looked wistfully into the kitchen, wondering if he'd ever hold Joan again, and how she'd take the news of his suicide. Paul watched his double, on high-speed rewind, absentmindedly stirring cream out of his coffee. Then Joan and the other Paul jumped out of their seats, the lights went out, and their footsteps retreated back toward the bedroom.

Paul rubbed his temples and walked toward his favorite easy chair. From the back of the house he heard the obnoxious klaxon of his alarm clock. It sounded very unbackward.

"Sorry, my friend." Rafe laughed. "The current has changed, and time is flowing forward again. We've got a busy day ahead of us."

Paul saw Joan shuffle into the kitchen and disappear behind the pantry door to get the coffee.

2

FEAR ATTACKS ONLY WEAKNESS, SO CONFRONT IT WITH STRENGTH

PAUL WATCHED FROM THE DOORWAY AS HIS IMAGE ENTERED THE kitchen. He hadn't noticed before that the small end of his necktie stuck out, and how pale he looked against the dark blue suit.

He watched himself sit down at the breakfast table as Joan joined him with two steaming cups of coffee. "Why don't you eat some breakfast, Paul? You've been living on coffee and junk food for weeks." He stirred the cereal but didn't take a bite. "You had nightmares again last night, didn't you?"

Paul blew across the coffee mug. "You know what they're going to do today, don't you?"

"Paul, you're exhausted. Call and tell them you can't make it today. Stay home. Tell them you're sick."

"I can't. I've got to get ready for that meeting at the bank this afternoon. I don't know what I'm going to do, but I have to do something. They're going to close the school.

FEAR IS A COWARD AND A LIAR.

IT WANTS TO SEE YOU WEAK,

BECAUSE ONLY THEN

CAN IT BE STRONG.

And you know what that means: we lose everything—my job, our house, everything."

"Not everything, Paul. We still have each other. And Jeff and Sandra. We've had to start all over before. The world can't throw any problem our way that God won't give us the strength to handle. Maybe it's all for the best this way. Maybe keeping the school just isn't worth all the stress and heartbreak."

Paul watched himself sip coffee, unsure whether to laugh or rage at the fact that not only was he having to relive this mental anguish, he was having to do it in duplicate. His image looked out the window. "It's too late for me to get a nine-to-five job. I'd never fit into a law firm, and with nothing but ten wasted years on my résumé, they'd never hire me. I used to think that one advantage of being my own boss was that nobody could fire me. Hah! What a joke. The truth is no one would hire me."

Standing off to the side, Rafe whispered to Paul, "Fear is a coward. It attacks when you are weak and confused. Like most cowards, though, fear is easily bluffed. It retreats when confronted by strength and deliberation. Fear never would have gotten to you like this a year ago, would it?"

Paul scowled at Rafe. "A year ago things were a lot different, a lot more certain."

"Yes, yes. That's how fear works. First it sends along doubt to soften you up. You begin to doubt whether or not you're doing things right. Then you doubt whether you're doing the right thing. And finally you doubt whether you're even the right person. Once there is enough doubt, once you stop believing in yourself, then fear knows it can defeat you. Its very cowardice is what makes fear such a treacherous enemy."

"The reason there is fear, Rafe, is that there are serious problems—problems I can't solve. There is no doubt that I am out of money. That is a fact. There is no doubt that when I stop making my mortgage payments, the bank will foreclose. That is a fact. And if I don't believe in myself anymore, it is those brutal, real facts that are responsible, not fear, not doubt, not the bogeyman."

"Fear is also a liar." Rafe spoke with the certainty of someone describing an ancient and familiar foe. "Fear will take a bundle of those things you call facts—each of which might even be true standing alone—and weave them into a picture that is totally false. By adding different facts, or by arranging them in a different way, you could paint a very different picture, couldn't you? One where everything works out for the best. But fear will never paint that picture for you, and will do everything possible to prevent you from painting it yourself.

"Fear will never tell you the truth. Fear wants you to be weak, because then it can be strong. When you are strong, fear cannot dominate you. By accepting fear's picture of a bleak future, you become a participant in a fraud—a fraud in which you are also the victim.

"To conquer this cowardly liar, you must confront it with strength and determination, and with the facts and the hope that it wishes to hide from you in the fog of despair. Do not listen to fear. Attack it."

3

FEAR IS A PRISON FROM WHICH
ACTION WINS FREEDOM

PAUL SMIRKED AT THE NOTION THAT FEAR WAS A COWARD AND A liar; what would fear be afraid of, and why would it lie? Rafe was speaking as though fear were a real living being, some sort of demon that could take physical possession of your body, make you do things you didn't want to do. Could it be that his fear really wasn't part of him but some external thing trying to work its way in from the outside?

"Have you ever seen the Great Wall of China?" Something in the way he said it convinced Paul that not only had Rafe seen the Great Wall, he'd watched it being built. "Like most such walls, it was much better at keeping people in than at keeping invaders out. The Great Wall was a prison wall. So is fear.

"Fear is a prison. It will no more keep frightening things out of your life than the Great Wall kept Mongol invaders out of China. But it can destroy your freedom of action so effectively that you can't do the things that could prevent what you fear from happening."

Paul's image looked at his watch and pushed away from the table. Joan wasn't ready to quit, though. "Why don't you call Bill Roberts? He might lend you money."

Paul snorted. "Roberts thinks I'm nuts for spending all my time with this school instead of making money. Nothing would give him more pleasure than to have me come begging for a handout."

"Then what about your father? He might give you a loan."

Paul rolled his eyes, remembering the early years when his father called almost every day with leads on a "real" job. "Dad's got his own problems. He doesn't need to have a failed son come asking for handouts."

"Then I'm going back to work."

"No way! The kids need you at home now, especially with Jeff having so much trouble at school."

"Well, Paul, just what *are* we going to do?"

Paul's image picked up his briefcase and refilled the coffee mug. When Joan put her hands on her hips, he knew it was time to exit. "Don't worry, honey, everything will be okay. It'll work out fine. The bank will give us a loan extension, but I do have to get into the office and get prepared for that meeting." Paul watched his image slink out of the kitchen toward the front door. Joan wiped her hands on her apron as she followed him out for a perfunctory kiss at the doorway.

"Are you telling Joan the truth, Paul, or is that just wishful thinking?" Paul marveled at Rafe's penchant for asking questions that permitted only one truthful answer.

POSITIVE THINKING IS
WORKING FOR SOMETHING AND
BELIEVING THAT IT WILL
HAPPEN.

WISHFUL THINKING IS WAITING
FOR SOMETHING AND HOPING
THAT IT WILL HAPPEN.

"I'm surprised at you, Rafe. Haven't you ever heard of the power of positive thinking?"

"Yes indeed. In fact I'd like to think that I played some small part in the writing of a book by that name. But do you know the distinction between positive thinking and wishful thinking?"

"Tell me."

"Positive thinking is believing that something will happen, wishful thinking is hoping it will happen. Positive thinking is working for something to happen, wishful thinking is waiting for it to happen.

"Wishful thinking is the lock that fear puts on the prison gate. You know the good-cop/bad-cop routine? Where the bad cop beats you up and then the good cop gets you to confess by treating you well? Well, fear is the bad cop, threatening you with doom and dread. But fear needs a good cop, or else you might just get frightened enough to do something constructive to chase fear away.

"So fear lets you indulge yourself for a while in flights of wishful thinking. Somehow, you think, something will happen to make the problems go away. By the time you wake up, it's too late. What you feared has happened, and fear has defeated you.

"The only way to escape from the prison of fear is action. You cannot wish your way out, you cannot wait your way out. You can only work your way out. Every time you escape the prison of fear, you grow stronger and more confident. It will always be there, trying to wall you in, but you will eventually grow so strong that you can just step right over the walls."

4

ANY HARM VIOLENCE CAN DO, FEAR CAN DO

OUT IN THE FRONT YARD RAFE AND PAUL WATCHED PAUL'S image gazing back at the house. "It is a lovely house," Paul said to Rafe, "more than I can afford, but it makes Joan happy. It doesn't really matter now, though, because we're going to lose it all anyway."

Rafe sniffed one of Joan's roses. "Fear is also a thief."

"Fear isn't going to steal my house, Rafe, the bank is."

Rafe looked firmly at Paul. "No, your fear is preventing you from admitting weakness, chancing rejection, and asking for help.

"Fear is stealing from you your freedom to act, your desire to succeed, your willingness to stick your neck out, even your capacity to care. Once it has stolen those things, it's only a matter of time before it takes your possessions as well."

Paul rolled his eyes. "Give me a break."

Rafe continued. "Fear is a killer, too."

UNDERSTAND YOUR FEAR, BUT
NEVER SURRENDER TO IT. THE
FIRST BACKWARD STEP CAN
CAUSE A DOWNWARD SPIRAL OF
PANIC, RETREAT, AND FAILURE.

"Oh, right. Fear is a coward. Fear is a liar. Fear is a prison. Fear is a thief. And now, fear is a killer."

"Sure, it happens all the time. There's a crash on Wall Street, someone panics and sells out at the bottom in reaction to fear's false presentation of the facts, loses everything, and then jumps out the window. First he let fear rob him of his money and then he let fear push him off the balcony.

"Fear, you see, can't hurt you by itself, because it's not even real. It needs a weapon, and the weapon fear most often wields is panic. Panic is simply an unreasoned reaction to fear. More often than not, panic is not only an inappropriate reaction, it actually causes the very thing of which you are afraid."

At that moment the children came out. Jeff, big for an eight-year-old, and strong, and Sandra, the six-year-old towhead. "Children," Rafe said, kneeling invisibly beside them, "fear is going to take your father tonight, perhaps. Be brave. Fear can't hurt you unless you let it." The children stopped for a moment, as though some exotic fragrance had touched their nostrils, hinting of distant lands to be explored. Then the school bus pulled up and they raced off, backpacks bouncing like pogo sticks.

Rafe stood silently watching the yellow bus round the corner. He looked like a man who had seen many children lose their fathers.

"Fear is a thief and a killer. Any harm someone else can do to you by violence, fear can cause by your reaction to it. But remember that fear is also a coward. It likes to work under the dark of doubt. Like other thieves and killers, fear shrinks away when you shine a light on it."

"Shine a light on it? How do you shine a light on fear?"

"You're leaving now," Rafe said as he hopped through the door into the backseat. The familiar backfire cracked the air as his image cranked up the engine. "Hop in the car and we'll talk at the office." Paul climbed in. He was getting used to not having to open the door.

5

Give Fear a Name and It
Becomes Just a Problem

THE SCHOOL WAS DESERTED WHEN THEY SHOWED UP; THE KIDS wouldn't arrive until eight thirty. Paul's image went straight to the office, removed the bank report from his briefcase, and started working the calculator with clumsy fingers. With every subtotal he grimaced as though experiencing actual physical pain. Rafe watched with the fascinated stare of a child examining a bug under a magnifying glass. "What's going on in his head right now?"

"How should I know?" Paul replied, causing Rafe to look at him with arched eyebrows. "Well, what I mean is that it's a pretty confused jumble in there. I guess he's mainly worried about money."

"Okay, so the problem is money," Rafe said. "What are some things you can do to raise money?"

"It's not that easy!" Paul shot back. "He's—I've—tried everything."

"Everything?"

"Just about. Most of these kids don't have parents who could pitch in, and I can't put them to work, because it's against the child labor laws."

"So the problem is changing the laws?"

"Oh, that would look great in the newspapers, wouldn't it? 'Noted child-welfare activist puts children to work in factories to raise money for his school.' "

"Okay, then what about Joan's suggestion to call Bill Roberts, or to ask your father for a loan?"

"Not on your life," Paul countered. "Roberts would string me out for as long as it amused him, then shoot me down. Dad would tell me to get a job."

Rafe rubbed his chin thoughtfully. "So the problem is learning to deal with rejection?"

"I deal with rejection just fine, thank you."

"What about Phyllis Nesserbaum over at New Trails Learning Center? Have you spoken with her?"

"How do you know about New Trails?" Paul asked suspiciously.

"Let's just say I get around. Don't they have money?"

"Rafe, they're the competition!"

"Competition? Aren't there enough troubled kids to go around?"

"Of course there are enough troubled kids, Rafe. There's not enough money. And Nesserbaum gets more than her share. Any help she gave me would come with a price tag—giving up control of my school."

"So the problem is trying to work with Phyllis without losing control?"

"I'm afraid that's a real problem, Rafe, trying to work with Phyllis without having her take over everything."

Rafe smiled. "If it's just a problem, Paul, then you don't need to be afraid. You may be unable to conquer fear, but you can always solve problems. If you give fear a name, then it becomes just a problem to be solved."

A loud *snap* punctured the silence as Paul's image cracked a pencil in half and flung the pieces across the room.

"We'd better go out before someone gets hurt," Rafe said. "Who knows what cosmic havoc might be created if your double killed you with a broken pencil." In the hallway Rafe took a drink from the cooler. "When you were in college, how come you decided not to jump out of that airplane at the last minute?"

"How do you know about that?"

"I told you, I get around. Was it the same reason you hate roller coasters?"

"Yeah."

"The same reason you keep your savings in a bank account instead of the stock market?"

"How do you . . . Never mind. Basically, Rafe, I'm a coward. The reason I have no glory is I have no guts."

"Now we know what fear calls you, Paul. It calls you coward. Of course you're not a coward. Prudent and risk-averse, perhaps to excess sometimes, but certainly not gutless. But when you allow fear to apply a label to you, you gradually assume that identity. With each new opportunity to take a risk, fear whispers into your ear, 'You can't do that. You're a coward.' And you nod in agreement. Isn't it true that despite all the risks you've taken in starting up the school, you see yourself as more 'cowardly' today than you did ten years ago?"

GIVE FEAR A NAME. TALK TO IT.

FORCE IT TO BE RATIONAL.

NAME YOUR FEAR AND IT

BECOMES JUST A PROBLEM. IT IS

EASIER TO SOLVE PROBLEMS

THAN IT IS TO CONQUER

NAMELESS FEAR.

"Well, yes, but—"

Rafe cut him off with a raised hand. "Saving money for the children has nothing to do with it, or you'd have gotten what you call 'a real job' long ago. The fact is you are beginning to accept the identity that fear wants to give you. Give fear a name and it becomes just a problem; let fear name you and *you* become the problem."

6

FEAR CREATES ENEMIES, COURAGE CREATES FRIENDS

RAFE AND PAUL WALKED OUT TO THE PLAYGROUND WHILE Paul's image continued to abuse his calculator. The first recess had started, and kids were attacking the jungle gym in imagined heroics.

Rafe leaned against a tetherball pole not currently in use. "Why are you afraid of Phyllis Nesserbaum?"

"I told you, Rafe, I'm not afraid of her. I compete with her. There are only so many people who donate to schools like this, and Phyllis has the inside track on the high-society high rollers. I'm not part of that scene."

"The high-society scene," Rafe asked, absentmindedly tossing the tetherball around the pole, "that's where the money is?"

Rafe and Paul noticed several kids looking wide-eyed in their direction, and realized that from their perspective the tetherball was spontaneously looping itself around the pole. "Come on," said Rafe, "let's go walk around a bit."

FEAR EXCLUDES AND CREATES
ENEMIES. COURAGE INCLUDES
AND CREATES FRIENDS.

"If your problem is money, then why are you afraid to go where the money is?"

Paul dug his hands into his pockets. "I'm not afraid. They're just not my kind of people."

Rafe's eyebrows went up again. "Oh, what kind of people are they?"

"Arrogant. They look down their long noses at me and my cheap tweed jacket. Life's just too short to be kissing up to . . ." The words trailed off as Paul looked back toward the children, his children, running around the playground.

"To the enemy?"

"Well, as a matter of fact, some of them are. They've tried to shut down my school for ten years, and now it looks like they're going to do it."

A basketball came rolling toward them through the grass, and Rafe kicked it back, greatly alarming the little boy who was chasing it. "I've got to stop doing that," Rafe reminded himself. "Maybe they just don't understand what you're trying to do."

"*You* don't understand, Rafe. They don't want to understand."

"Yes," Rafe replied, "fear does that to people."

"Fear? They're not afraid of me."

"Are you sure?" Rafe stopped and looked at Paul. "If you took a bunch of your kids to their front doors one evening singing Christmas carols, would they come out to see you?"

"Good point."

Rafe stopped under the big oak tree and pulled a handful of peanuts out of his pocket. He stopped to feed a pair of gray squirrels, and for a moment seemed to be aware of nothing else in the world. As they ran off full-cheeked, he said, "That's another way fear destroys you."

"Excuse me?" Paul's attention was still with the squirrels scampering up the tree.

"Remember how I said that your reaction to fear can cause you to lose all your possessions, even to lose your life? Well, another way fear can destroy you is by creating enemies.

"Fear wants to keep out anyone who's different, who makes you feel the least bit uncomfortable, anyone who challenges your established opinions and assumptions. At the same time that your fear is excluding them, their fear is excluding you. Pretty soon, they're not just different, they're worse. And of course, you're not just different to them, you're worse, too. And it's not a very big step from being worse to being wrong. And from being wrong it's not a very big step to being an enemy.

"Fear excludes and creates enemies. It takes great courage to bring down the walls of exclusion and reach out to people who are different from you."

"Yeah, that sounds nice, Rafe, but in the real world there's a lot of risk in trying to reach out and touch everyone. Trusting an enemy is the best way in the world to lose everything you have."

"Everything?" Rafe replied. "Not everything, Paul, it's not everything at all once you see the big picture."

7

Fear Gets Lost
in the Big Picture

Paul's image slammed on the brakes and cursed at the old man who had cut him off. It was their third close call since leaving the school. "You know," Rafe chirped, "if this is the way you always drive, you're a lot luckier than I gave you credit for."

"Very funny. I may be afraid of losing my school, and I may be afraid of rich people, but at least when I get behind the wheel of a car, I'm a man above fear."

"There are times, my friend, when a little fear is a good thing," Rafe replied with a laugh. "In fact a little fear can be quite a positive thing if it helps you see the big picture. Come on, let's go for a walk."

"Right now? We can't go for a walk! We're headed for the bank."

"Oh, no problem." Rafe pulled the watch out of his pocket and pushed a button; instantly everything froze in place. Rafe stepped out, motioning Paul to follow him

AS LONG AS YOU'RE STILL
BREATHING, YOU HAVEN'T LOST
EVERYTHING.

through the door. They walked down a narrow alley. Paul was fascinated that even though time had stopped, he could still smell the garbage. Halfway down the alley Rafe stopped and looked at a man sleeping under a makeshift blanket of newspapers. An empty booze bottle protruded from a brown bag near his head. "Is this what you mean by losing everything?" Rafe asked.

"Close enough!"

"Okay, take a look." An image appeared on the brick wall in front of them, as though a rear-screen projection television had been installed there. Two men were standing on a stage; one was giving the other a large plaque and speaking.

"Jack O'Mara was down, but he never let himself get counted out. He pulled himself out of the gutter, and somehow God gave him the courage to quit drinking. And now not a day goes by that Jack isn't out there in the streets helping others who are down, showing them how to get back up. Let's give a big hand . . ."

As the picture faded out, Paul saw tears tracking the deep wrinkles of Jack's ruddy cheeks. He looked down at the younger man on the ground, who appeared so much older than he would in the future. Rafe stooped to place another layer of newspaper over Jack's shoulders. "I guess as long as you're still breathing, you haven't lost everything."

They walked on through the alley and across the street. An old man and a young boy were sitting together at the bus stop. "Come on," Rafe motioned, "let's go listen in for a minute."

The little boy was talking: "Everybody says you used to be rich. Were you really?"

The old man laughed indulgently. "If you mean did I have a lot of money, yes I used to be rich. I had a big car, and a man to drive it, and in the morning people would say 'good-day' real polite because they were all so scared of me." The man looked at the little boy and winked. "Oh, I was pretty tough in those days. Used to yell and scream a lot, and treated some people pretty bad. But I made a lot of money."

"Wow!" The little boy's eyes were big and greedy. "What happened?"

The old man frowned and shook his head. "Well, it just sort of all fell apart. There were lots of reasons, but mostly I just got tired. The business went downhill faster than I could catch it."

The little boy narrowed his gaze. "You must really be sad now, huh?" The old man laughed. "This morning I'm sitting here with a delightful young man. Then I'll go read at the library for a while, and feed the squirrels in the park. When I get back home, the wonderful woman who put up with me for so many years will have soup on the stove, and she'll jump when I pinch her bottom like she didn't know it was coming, even though I've done it every day for thirty-six years." The little boy blushed and looked away, and the old man tussled his hair. "No, I reckon I'm not sad."

Rafe froze the scene again and they walked back toward the car. Paul was getting used to Rafe's hand on his shoulder. "I guess you don't really mean you could lose everything, do you?"

"I know," Paul muttered, "keep your perspective. There

are still children starving in India even though I cleaned my plate all those years. But it's easy enough for you to pick out those happy endings. What about all the endings that aren't so happy?"

8

〜〜

FEAR IS MANY TOMORROWS, COURAGE IS ONE TODAY

RAFE WAS QUIET FOR A LONG WHILE. PAUL COULD SEE THE BANK building looming up ahead. Finally Rafe broke the silence. "Who said anything about endings?"

"What? What endings?"

"You accused me of only picking out happy endings. Do you think Jack O'Mara will never struggle with the bottle again after his award? Or that the old man and his wife won't know loss and loneliness? There's only one ending in life, and whether it's happy or sad depends on your perspective."

"So why didn't you take me to those days? To Jack O'Mara fighting to keep his sanity, or that old man weeping over the loss of his wife? That would have given me a whole different—perspective—wouldn't it?"

"Not really, Paul, because even though Jack must always struggle, the struggle always makes him stronger. And even though the old man lives his last years alone, he finds his

DON'T GET CRUSHED BETWEEN

THE ANVIL OF YESTERDAY'S

REGRETS AND THE HAMMER OF

TOMORROW'S WORRIES.

own inner peace through his loneliness. Remember how I said that I can see time the way an eagle in the sky looks down upon the railroad tracks? Well, from that perspective there really are no endings at all. Every time you round a corner or enter a tunnel and think that it's an ending, I know that you could just as well call it a beginning. Or a middle."

Paul's image was cursing the lack of parking spaces in the garage. Finally he pulled into the handicapped stall, looking both ways to make sure no one was watching. Rafe and Paul followed him toward the building.

"You see, Paul, fear is worrying about all the different tomorrows. Fear is worrying about the bad days that may or may not come, and even worrying about the good ones because you know they can't last. You can dream of the future, plan for it—those are good things to do—but you can't control all the tomorrows. You'll have some good ones, and you'll have some bad ones."

Paul's image looked at his watch and fidgeted while they waited for the elevator. Rafe looked at the two Pauls and smiled. "The more vividly you anticipate the bad days, the more certain you can be they will come. I think we're about to see something like that happen now."

The elevator door opened, revealing a cab jammed full of people. The door closed, leaving Paul's image standing outside. He kicked the door with a curse and glared again at his watch as if by sheer force of will he could stop the flow of time. Then he stalked off toward the staircase.

Rafe and Paul hurried to follow Paul's image down the stairs. Paul smiled to himself, knowing that right now his image was anticipating that the door would be locked at the

COURAGE IS TO STOP
WORRYING ABOUT ALL THE
POSSIBLE TOMORROWS AND THE
TROUBLE THEY MIGHT BRING,
AND TO GIVE YOUR WHOLE
ATTENTION TO THE ONE TODAY
IN WHICH YOU ALWAYS LIVE.

bottom. *What if I could tell him—tell myself—that it's really not locked?* Paul wondered. How much wasted energy we could save. They followed Paul's image through the lobby toward the conference room.

"To be afraid is to live among all the many frightening tomorrows as if they were certain to happen. To be courageous is to close off all those tomorrows and devote your attention and energy to the one today that is the only thing you ever experience with certainty."

Rafe stopped Paul for a minute. Without a word he extended his arm toward the crowded bank lobby. It was an obvious message: Most of the people were only partially there. Their minds were elsewhere. Many of them appeared frightened, Paul noted as he looked more closely.

"Another way people frighten themselves is by creating many imaginary tomorrows in which everything is all right, into which they can escape from the pain and uncertainty of dealing with today. Either way, living among the many possible tomorrows will distract your attention from how you must think, feel, and act on this one today in order to pursue your purpose with courage."

Paul's image opened the conference room door, stood for a moment like Daniel at the mouth of the lion's den, then went in. "Let's go see how you do with *this* today," Rafe said, bringing a reluctant Paul along with him.

9

FEAR IS A REACTION, COURAGE IS A DECISION

RAFE AND PAUL STOOD OFF TO THE SIDE, WHERE THEY WERE framed by a pair of oil paintings of paunchy old men with muttonchop sideburns who seemed very satisfied with their own importance. Everything about the room was designed to intimidate: the walnut paneling, the ornate chandelier, the granite fireplace, the massive conference table. Sitting across the table from the bankers and lawyers, Paul's image was clearly intimidated. "Well, Mr. Peterson . . ." the senior loan officer began.

Paul knew that when Marty Weatherford used such formality, it was going to be a tough meeting. With his short hair and powerful build, Marty looked more like a Marine than a banker. Paul had first met Marty through Rotary, and now they tried to play racquetball together on Thursdays.

"It seems that your business—"

"It's a school," Paul's image snapped. "It's not my business, it's a school for kids who would otherwise be out on the street, or in jail. Or dead."

Marty sighed dramatically. "Well, yes, of course it's a school, but perhaps if you'd run it more like a business, you wouldn't be having these problems today." He whispered a question to the man sitting next to him, and in response was handed a folder.

"Now, according to our records, Mr. Peterson, you are three months behind in making payments on the school-building loan, and your debt ratios have all fallen below the accepted—"

Paul cut him off by drilling an exclamation point into the table with his finger. "You know well and good that I will pay off that loan, Marty! For crying out loud, you've got my house as collateral. I'll catch up on the payments, I just need some more time to work things out."

Marty gave Paul a "this is going to hurt me more than it's going to hurt you" look, then closed his briefcase. "I'm sorry, Paul, but you know as well as I do that you're behind on house payments as well. I'm afraid we have no choice. We're going to have to foreclose on both loans. I'm sorry."

Paul's image exploded out of the chair. "*You're* afraid! You don't even know what the word means." Although the breadth of a solid mahogany table was between them, Marty and the other bank officers backed off defensively as Paul's image erupted. "And you don't know the meaning of the word *sorry*, either! What am I supposed to do now? Take my family and my students and go live under a bridge somewhere?"

Paul watched himself rage at his friend. At that moment, he saw how malignant fear could be. It wasn't Marty's responsibility to pay off his loans, yet he was screaming as though his friend and banker had hurt one of his children. In fact Marty was right. Paul didn't have a clue how he would pay off those loans.

"Did you see how fear changed the subject?" Rafe asked as Paul's image subsided into a despondent slump in the leather conference room chair. Paul shook his head.

"Fear rejects criticism, especially when it's legitimate. Rather than facing up to the problem in a mature, rational way, it uses anger and guilt and self-pity to refocus the discussion. It doesn't want to hear about those things that you aren't doing but should be doing and instead wants to blame someone else for your predicament."

Security guards had come into the room from both doors, but Marty waved them back. "Everything's okay now. Perhaps someone could just escort Mr. Peterson to his car."

Paul's image snapped his briefcase shut. "I don't need an escort. I know the way."

Rafe gave Paul a nudge. "We'd better hurry if we're going to keep up with your friend. Let's take a shortcut." Rafe pulled Paul through the wall into the teller's cage, and then right through the counter into the lobby. Paul's image was steaming around the corner, knocking people out of his way as he went.

"Look at that face," Rafe said. "All that anger, you'd never know that he is running away scared." The two fell in behind as Paul's image plowed through the front door.

"Of course he's scared," Paul said defensively, rather embarrassed at the performance that looked so much more

THE MOST POWERFUL STEPS YOU

CAN TAKE TO CONQUER FEAR

ARE TO TAKE PERSONAL

RESPONSIBILITY FOR YOUR OWN

LIFE AND TO REFRAIN FROM

BLAMING OTHERS FOR YOUR

TROUBLES AND FAILURES.

outrageous seen from the outside than it had from the inside. "He's about to lose everything—he should be scared."

"Everything?" smiled Rafe.

"Don't give me that 'perspective' crap again, Rafe. This is an impossible situation and you know it."

Just ahead they watched Paul's image slam his briefcase down onto the hood of the car and rip the parking ticket out from under the windshield wiper. He threw his briefcase across the seat, got in, and slammed his fist onto the dashboard.

"It's not impossible, Paul. You just haven't yet decided to have the courage to deal with it like a problem instead of reacting to it like a threat.

"Fear is the parent of both cowardice and courage. Which child will you choose to raise?"

10

WITH FAITH
FEAR BECOMES AN ALLY

THE CHEVY RATTLED ACROSS THE GRAVEL PARKING LOT AND backfired loudly as Paul's image turned off the ignition. He rested his forehead against the steering wheel for a long moment, then left the keys in the car and climbed out. From the backseat Rafe and Paul watched him climb the hill toward the cliffs.

"Am I going to jump?" Paul asked as his image disappeared over the crest of the hill.

Rafe smiled softly. "Don't you know?"

"I do know that at this very moment I—the 'I' that is up there watching the sun go down—intend to end it."

Rafe stopped smiling and looked at Paul so intensely that he turned away. "Do you want him to jump, Paul?"

Paul licked his thumb and tried to rub a peanut butter stain out of the backseat. "I don't know. I don't want him . . . I don't want to die, but I can't go on like this. Fear

PRAY FOR FAITH. COURAGE

WILL COME AS AN ADDED

BENEFIT.

may be a treacherous enemy like you said, Rafe, and if that's so, then it has beaten me. I do want it to end."

Rafe looked more closely at Paul, then climbed out of the car. Motioning with his head for Paul to follow, he ascended the path. The sun illuminated the evening sky as if it were God's own stained-glass cathedral. Paul watched his image's hair blowing in the breeze at the edge of the cliff.

"You can't see it, can you?"

Paul blinked. "See what?"

"See fear standing behind you there, preparing to shove you off that cliff. You can't see it, can you?"

"No, I can't see it, Rafe."

"You can't see it because it's not there. It's nothing, not even a puff of hot air. Just a figment of your imagination, yet you're about to be pushed to your death by it."

The sun touched the horizon and continued its descent. The man at the edge stared straight into the light and wrapped his arms around his shoulders as though trying to stay warm against a winter wind. "You see, Paul," Rafe continued, "that man out there can't take his mind off all those depressing tomorrows. If he just had faith, then fear could become his ally."

Now only the top quarter of the sun gleamed above the horizon, sending a sword of brilliant orange across the waves, its tip pointed directly at the man on the cliff. Paul was losing his concentration to a morbid fascination with the scene unfolding before him: Was he about to watch his own suicide? He had to force himself to process Rafe's last words. "How can fear be an ally?"

NEVER QUIT

Rafe looked at Paul, but the young man's eyes were riveted on the figure silhouetted in the setting sun.

"If you have faith, there is nothing to fear. Believe in the meaning of life and your own purpose in life, and fear simply becomes a warning that you are not yet prepared for the challenge. Master your fear and it becomes an ally."

The sun's last fragment floated for a moment on the sea, a jeweled ring on the hand of an elfin princess, then it dipped below the surface.

Paul's image moved closer to the edge. At that second the splendor of the fiery orange sky seemed to suck the air right off the hilltop. It was as if every ounce of beauty from everywhere in the universe had been packed into that one ultimate sunset. At the cliff the other Paul's hands fell to his sides.

Paul wanted to scream, to yank his image back away from the precipice, but he was frozen in horror.

The man on the edge took a step and leaned forward into the wind. Instantly the hill was vacant. No Rafe. No sound. No air. Paul was yanked off his feet and sent hurtling toward the sunset. At the edge of the cliff, as though he had slammed into an invisible wall, he was wrenched violently downward. He saw his own flailing body coming at him from below and knew that the two would reconnect at the moment of impact.

"Raaaaafe!"

11

STICK TO YOUR PURPOSE

"PAUL. PAUL! WAKE UP. WHAT'S THE MATTER?"

The screams were still echoing through the dark caverns of Paul's fading subconscious mind. His pajamas were soaked, he clutched his pillow like a lifeline. The sensation of falling had stopped abruptly, but there was no impact. Just the feel of Joan's hand on his shoulder and her voice in his ear.

"It's okay, Paul, it's just a dream. Just a bad dream."

Paul opened his eyes. By what right was he back in his own bedroom? "What time is it?"

"It's not even six yet. Try to get some more sleep, okay?"

Paul tried to lurch out of bed, but Joan pressed him back down. Too exhausted to fight, he closed his eyes and tried to put it all together. It couldn't have been a dream. It was too real. Maybe heaven was lying in bed with Joan snuggled against his back, knowing he'd never fall again.

"Paul?"

IF YOU'RE NOT ENJOYING THE
JOURNEY, YOU PROBABLY WON'T
ENJOY THE DESTINATION.

"Hmmm?"

"Who's Rafe?"

"What do you mean, who's Rafe?"

"You were talking in your sleep and said that name a lot. You were screaming it when I woke you up."

Paul just groaned and tried to push himself up, but Joan pressed down against his shoulder as he tried to rise. "Paul, it's not even six o'clock yet. You don't have to get up. Sometimes the most important thing you can do is resist the temptation to do something when it would be more valuable just to stop for a while."

Paul surrendered to Joan's touch, sinking back into the bed. Eyes closed, his mind teetered between consciousness and sleep. "Rafe? Rafe?" No answer. In the lonely darkness fear held him trapped. Today was the day he would lose it all. The school, the bank, the cliff all came back to him as powerfully as a memory of something that had already happened —a memory of the future. He drifted off to sleep with the fear of falling again paralyzing his will even to crawl out of bed.

"Give what a name, Paul?"

Joan shook Paul's shoulder softly, dragging him back out of the nightmare confrontation with fear.

"You were talking again, saying 'give it a name,' as if it were urgent."

Paul stretched and looked at the clock. It was nearly seven. "I don't know, just a dream, I guess."

"Don't go to work yet, Paul. Let's take a walk, like we used to do in the mornings. It's been too long since we really talked."

As they walked, Paul's breathing untied the knots in his

DON'T BE IMPRISONED BY

GOALS THAT YOU HAVE

OUTGROWN.

stomach. How long had it been since he'd really heard the birds' morning songs, smelled the fresh new air? Then, like an unwanted intruder, the familiar voice reminded him: *Today is the day you lose everything.*

"Joan, I haven't really been honest with you."

"How so?"

"I've been keeping up a brave face for you and the kids, but I don't see how we're going to make it. Today the bank's going to take everything away from us. I'm afraid the dream is over."

Joan stopped and looked out across the bay. One of the reasons they had built in this area was the morning stillness of the woods. "Paul, the dream ended a long time ago."

Paul stiffened, not sure whether to be annoyed or angered. "What are you talking about? We turned that old warehouse into a real school, we've got nearly two hundred kids enrolled—and if it weren't for running out of money, we could keep growing."

"Think back to those days in law school, Paul. You weren't dreaming of becoming an administrator, a fund-raiser, a bureaucrat. Your dream was to spend time with kids who had problems, to help them cope in a hard world. Sure, you've got the school now, and we've got a nice house, but you almost never spend time with the kids anymore. Not our kids or the kids at the school. You're always in meetings or working on budgets."

"But that's not the same. What I'm doing—"

Joan's raised hand cut him off. "Your cause is noble, but anyone who looked at what you actually do every day would scarcely be able to distinguish you from all your classmates with their jobs in law practices and corporate offices. For the little contact you have with kids, you could just as well get some high-paying job and donate the money to hire a manager for the school. Your dream is dead, Paul. It's been dead for a long time."

Paul looked down at the little picnic area where they used to take the schoolkids before classes got so big and budgets so tight. "My God." Paul sat on a park bench, cradling his head in his hands. "How did I get so far off track?"

Joan lifted his chin. "That's the wrong question. The right question is, how can you get back on track?"

"Okay, how can I get back on track?"

"Your dream is to help kids, right?"

Paul nodded.

"Well, how about instead of packing up your briefcase and rushing off to the office, you go home and spend some time with Sandra and Jeff. Maybe give them a ride to school. If you listen, I bet your kids will have some good ideas."

12

GIVE YOURSELF PERMISSION

"THE ANSWER'S SIMPLE, DADDY."

The warm sun, singing birds, and happy afterglow of rolling around on the grass tickling each other made Paul want to believe that his gap-toothed little daughter had the answer, but it was a struggle to prevent laughter from spoiling the seriousness of her moment at the podium.

"In that case, Pumpkin, I've been a dunce for waiting so long to ask you. What's the answer?"

"You got to get merpission, so you can do what you want to do."

"Merpission?"

"She means 'permission,' Dad," said Jeff, in between the karate kicks he was laying into enemies seen only by him.

"I need permission?"

"Yeth," Sandra exclaimed through the hole that was once home to front teeth. "Whenever I want to do something I want to do, I have to get merpission. Then I can do it. So

GIVE YOURSELF PERMISSION TO
BECOME THE PERSON YOU WERE
MEANT TO BE, AND TO STOP
TRYING TO BE THE PERSON
YOU THINK OTHERS
EXPECT YOU TO BE.

you just need to get someone to give you merpission. Then you can stop worrying and just go play with the kids. Like you want to do."

"But Pumpkin, I'm a grown-up. Who's gonna give me merpission?"

Sandra shrugged, cocked her head, and grinned. "I don't know, Daddy! Who tells you what to do?"

"Well, lots of people tell me what to do. But mostly, I guess, I do the things that I tell myself I should do."

Jeff pirouetted a roundhouse kick in his father's direction, missing his head by about six inches. A quick one-two punch, then he said with authority, "Well, then, you just have to ask yourself for permission."

"Ask myself for permission?"

"Sure! If you want to stop doing boring stuff and start doing fun stuff, who else do you need to ask?"

Deep in the back of his mind Paul thought he heard a metallic clang, like the noise of an iron bolt being thrown open on a prison door. Or maybe it was the sound of a spotlight switched on to sweep its rays across all the dark places where fear hides. Was it only yesterday that Rafe had stood on this very spot telling Paul's children that this night they might become fatherless?

"Well?" Paul arranged his facial expression to convey the seriousness with which he was considering this proposition. "Don't you think that maybe I should ask Mom for permission, too?"

"Oh, Daddy!" Sandra jumped into Paul's lap, nearly knocking him over, and put her jack-o'-lantern smile inches from his. "You know that Mommy will give you merpission to do anything you want to do."

13

DREAM EMOTIONALLY, THINK RATIONALLY

PAUL AND JOAN LEANED AGAINST THE CHEVY AND HELD HANDS as they watched the kids run off toward their classes. Ruthie Howard, one of the moms who volunteered at Shay's Point, had agreed to open things up at Paul's school that morning.

"I don't understand you." Paul turned his eyes from the playground equipment he knew he'd never be able to afford for Shay's Point toward Joan. "One minute you tell me to think big, and the next you tell me to be reasonable. One minute you tell me that my only limits are self-imposed, and the next you tell me to go easy on myself because I'm only human. Why, if I didn't love you so much, I might even accuse you of being inconsistent."

Joan smiled and yanked the short end of Paul's necktie, pulling it tight. "Well, my dear, you'd be wrong. I'm perfectly consistent."

"How do you explain that?"

"Easy. You need to be emotional on the upside and rational on the downside."

"Okay, psych major, can you put that into terms a dumb lawyer can understand?"

"It won't be easy, but I'll try. Let's see. Wherefore and whereas the beginning of any difficult enterprise requires an extraordinary amount of optimism and positive attitude, any party planning to undertake such difficult enterprise must imbue it with emotional energy at a level for which no rational explanation is possible. In the course of fulfilling the difficult enterprise, however, there will be unanticipated difficulties—elsewise such enterprise should not have been labeled difficult by the party of the first place. Such difficulties—also known as obstacles, hindrances, obstructions, barriers, or setbacks—may plunge the party of the first place into a state of melancholy—also known as depression—against which emotional energy and positive attitudes alone will not prevail. In such cases the party of the first place must exercise and practice disciplined thinking, which is based upon an objective search for facts and sober analysis of such facts, thus and thereby preventing the party of the first place from wallowing in unwarranted self-recrimination, overestimating the magnitude of obstacles, and overlooking possible alternative solutions to said difficulties. And so forth and so on."

"Very impressive, counselor! Intimidating, without informing. You would have made a great lawyer. But can you say it in English?"

Joan looked at him with a patience earned through years of working with children. "When explanation doesn't

EFFECTIVE ENTHUSIASM IS THE
MARRIAGE OF EMOTIONAL
ENERGY AND DISCIPLINED
INTELLECT. LIKE HAVING
COURAGE, WHETHER OR NOT
WE HAVE ENTHUSIASM IS A
PERSONAL CHOICE.

work, try example. That's what my mother always told me."

"Rafe said that very same thing," Paul blurted out without thinking, earning a look that notified him Joan intended to know everything about Rafe before day's end.

"When we were just starting up the school, nobody believed it was possible except you and me. And I only believed in the school because I believed in you. If you had been what you lawyers call a reasonable man back then, you would have listened to all those other reasonable people and gotten a real job. But you were unreasonable because you had a dream, a calling. You didn't have anything going for you except your passion, your emotional commitment to this cause. Shay's Point School was built on your emotional energy, Paul. That energy turned a dream into reality.

"But reality is more complicated than dreams, and emotions aren't enough to keep things going. In fact they can be downright harmful. Things start to go wrong, and instead of trying rationally to understand the problem, you blame yourself. Instead of asking for help, you try to do it all yourself, like you always have.

"This morning you said we might lose everything today. That was your emotions doing the talking. A little bit of rational thinking will show you that's not true, and guide you toward actions you can take to keep it from happening."

Paul put his hands around Joan's waist and pulled her close. "You are an amazing person, you know that? And I'm very lucky to have you as a partner in this life."

"Yes, you are."

"Sandra told me this morning that I just need to give myself permission to be happy. If I give myself permission to dream new dreams, can I have yours also?"

Joan smiled and touched his chin. "Let's do it together."

14

❧

ACCEPT ADVERSITY
AND IT BECOMES A TEACHER

AT THE OFFICE PAUL DIDN'T EVEN PULL THE FINANCIAL REPORTS and calculator out of his briefcase. Joan was right: All the enthusiasm and emotional energy in the world would not turn red ink black. Instead he drew a straight line down the center of a legal pad. At the top of one column he wrote the word *Problem*. At the top of the other he wrote *Cause*.

The first problem was easy: "Insufficient money." In the "Cause" column, Paul wrote that fewer people were contributing to the school because so many competing charities had sprung up, all clamoring for the shrinking donor pie.

No, that's not true, Paul thought, scratching through the words and looking out the window at the children on the playground. *The real reason we don't have enough money is that I don't like to raise money. I'd much rather be down at the courthouse befriending a kid in trouble or coming up with plans for a new program at the school. It makes me feel mercenary to*

ADVERSITY IS A QUIET TEACHER.
YOU MUST PROBE IT FOR THE
MEANING IT CONTAINS, AND
INTERPRET THE SUBTLE ANSWERS
WITH WHICH IT WILL RESPOND.

ask people for money, so I've relied for too long on the original backers. While Phyllis Nesserbaum and her type were out courting the money, I've been doing more pleasant things. And now I'm paying the price.

Paul turned back and wrote down the second problem: "Failed the bank audit." Then he set down his pen and spoke out loud. "We failed the audit because I'm so disorganized as an administrator, and because I delegated too much work to untrained volunteers without giving them adequate supervision."

Paul entered as problem number three "Not having allies in the community." *We don't have allies because I'm basically a fighter, not a bridge builder. Because I'm a pretty good fighter, there are a lot of bruised opponents out there who wouldn't mind seeing me take a fall.*

Yesterday Rafe had said that adversity is a quiet teacher; you only learn when you ask it questions. Paul was wondering what questions he should be asking this particular adversity when Ruthie stuck her head in the doorway. "Sorry to bother you, but there's a Phyllis Nesserbaum on the phone for you. Should I tell her you'll call back?"

"No, I'll take it, Ruthie. Thanks."

Paul looked back at his list before he picked up the phone. Phyllis Nesserbaum didn't have any of those problems because she didn't have any of the underlying causes. Paul pictured her behind her big desk, and felt smaller than he ever had.

"Hey, Phyllis. What's new?"

"Hello, Paul. I know this is awfully short notice, but if you don't have lunch plans today, I wonder if we can get together and talk about something?"

Paul checked his watch—ten thirty.

"Can it wait until tomorrow? I've got a pretty important meeting this afternoon."

There was a long silence, followed by a voice that didn't sound like it belonged to someone sitting behind a big desk. "Look, Paul, I know we haven't always seen eye to eye—you're probably laughing at the understatement of the year. But I think we also have a lot of respect for each other; I know I do for you. I'll level with you. I really have a problem. I need your help. I've got a board meeting tonight, and it would help me a lot if we could talk before then."

Paul could hardly believe his ears. Phyllis Nesserbaum had a problem? This should be interesting. "Where do you want to meet?"

"How about at Franco's, downtown?"

"Sounds good. Noon?"

"Super. I'll see you then. And I owe you one, Paul."

"We'll see. Take care."

Paul cradled the phone and looked back out the window at the now-vacant playground. Then he turned back to his legal pad and drew a line downward along the right side. At the top of this newly created third column he wrote the word "Solution." He sat for a long time staring at the page. At last he picked up his pen and in big letters filled in the new column with the words "GET HELP."

15

OBSTACLES ARE WHAT YOU SEE WHEN YOU TAKE YOUR EYES OFF YOUR GOALS

THE BELL SOUNDED ENDING FOURTH PERIOD. PAUL HAD ABOUT thirty minutes before he had to leave to meet Phyllis. He looked at the telephone as if it were a scorpion sitting on his desk. For ten years he had dreaded making this call. It was time, though. Paul closed his eyes and took a breath. "Dear God, I know it seems like I only pray when I'm in trouble. Please be with us both during this call, and guide me to say the right things."

Paul knew his father had been sitting in the dining room of his apartment, because he answered the phone on the first ring. "Hi, Dad."

"Hey, Paul! Great to hear ya. How're the kids?"

"They're great, Dad. Joan and I thought we'd have you over for dinner on Sunday. It's been too long."

"Love to. Tell you what, I'll make one of my famous raspberry pies. You should see how plump and juicy those berries are!"

KEEP A FOCUS ON YOUR REAL
GOALS BY CREATING A MENTAL
IMAGE OF THEIR ACHIEVEMENT
SO REAL AND TANGIBLE THAT
THEY BECOME MEMORIES OF
THE FUTURE.

"Sounds great, Dad. The kids will love it. Listen, I can't talk long, but I'm afraid I have some bad news."

Paul's father didn't interrupt the silence, so he continued.

"Things haven't been too good at the school lately—big-time money problems. I've got a meeting with the bank this afternoon. I think they're going to foreclose the mortgage on the school. Probably the one on the house, too. Kind of funny, huh, Dad? Here I am thirty-six years old and still bouncing checks."

"It happens. Will the bank extend you credit or let you pay interest-only for a while?"

"They already did that, Dad. I'm afraid we're talking fiscal rigor mortis here."

"What about your big donors? Could they help? Or maybe the public schools. You know, you really take a burden off of them. They ought to pitch in when you need help."

"Listen, Dad, it's really too late. That's all stuff I know I should have done, or done better, a long time ago. But at two o'clock the bank's gonna shut me down. And you know what? It's probably for the best."

"Obstacles are what you see when you take your eyes off your goals."

Every time it was as though Henry Ford's old aphorism was a freshly unearthed diamond. "I remember the first time you told me that, Dad. I still didn't make the track team, and Becky Johnson never went out with me."

"Those weren't your goals, Paul. You went to law school and married Joan. Those were your *real* goals. And now you're doing something with your life to make a difference. That takes a lot of courage."

Paul laughed. "Sometimes, Dad, the line between courageous and crazy is pretty fuzzy, and which side you're on is only evident in retrospect."

"Well, of course you're crazy, Paul, but you always have been. Runs in the family. But you're also brave as hell. You know, your mother was very proud of you. And I am, too."

"I know, Dad. Thanks."

Paul's father cleared his throat, the way he always did when he had something important to say but wasn't sure quite how to say it. Paul waited, not terribly displeased at the prospect of being late for Phyllis Nesserbaum. He had a good excuse.

"When your mother was ill, we decided to put her life insurance proceeds into a rainy-day fund. It's not very much. It was twenty-five thousand dollars four years ago, and to tell the truth I haven't looked at a statement since, but it's something higher than that now. Sounds to me like you've got weather problems at the school."

Paul couldn't remember the last time he had cried. "Yeah, Dad, the roof's leaking pretty bad."

"You still at First National?"

"At least until two o'clock."

"Okay. I'm gonna call Burt right now and have him make the transfer into your account so that it's there by two. I hope the weather clears up soon."

16

DON'T GO IT ALONE

PAUL'S ELATION BARELY LASTED TILL HE GOT OUT OF THE PARK-
ing lot. His father had bailed him out, but even so, within a
few months he'd be back in the same boat. Worse, he
would be living with a sense of obligation that he might
never be able to pay off.

Franco's was a cozy Italian place near the college. It was
a popular spot for business lunches because the food was
good, and it was one of the few places downtown that
didn't allow smoking. Phyllis was already there at a window
table.

They both ordered iced tea and the daily special. Phyllis
spoke first. "Marty Weatherford tells me you play racquetball. We should play sometime."

"I play, but I'm not very good at it."

"That's not what Marty says."

"How do you know Marty?"

"Before he joined First National, he was my banker at Bank-Star. Nice guy, isn't he?"

What else did he tell you about me, or my school? Paul wanted to ask. "We're both on tight schedules, so we should probably get down to business."

Phyllis cleared her throat and twisted her wedding ring. It was the first time he'd noticed it, but he was certain that Phyllis, the master networker, knew *his* wife's birthday, and probably even her shoe size.

"You might already know that our recent fund-raising campaign was very successful."

"That hurts." Paul smiled.

"I'm sorry, I didn't mean it to be invidious. The truth is, sometimes having too much money can bring even bigger problems than not having enough."

"I'd sure like to find out. Do you suppose the Community Foundation would give me a grant to study the problems of having too much money?"

Phyllis smiled. "Why not?"

Paul returned the smile. "What shall we call it? How about 'A Proposal to Study the Effects of Unearned Affluence on Middle-Aged Males'?"

Phyllis shook her head, still smiling. "Just because you don't have it doesn't mean you haven't earned it. Life's not always fair that way." The waiter laid out their spaghetti, and Paul ate while Phyllis talked.

"Part of the reason we've been so successful with our fund-raising is that we've got some new people on our board, real movers and shakers. They want a new vision, big plans for the future. They're really pushing me on it. You know, I'm a pretty good manager, and I really love

SIMPLIFY YOUR LIFE BY DOING

WHAT YOU'RE GOOD AT AND

GETTING HELP FOR WHAT

YOU'RE NOT GOOD AT.

what I do. But I also know my limits. I'm not a visionary leader. I leave that for people like you."

Paul twirled his spaghetti. "Well, I'm not sure if I'm a visionary leader, but lately I've also been learning a lot about my limitations. For example, I'm a damn lousy manager."

"You want my honest opinion, Paul? Watching you try to manage that school is like watching someone buy a Ferrari and then use it to drive to the corner market. I know you love those kids, but for you to be balancing the checkbook is a waste of a God-given talent. You inspire people, Paul, and you have vision. The world's got plenty of managers. We need more leaders. There are plenty of troubled kids to go around. We ought to be working together, not fighting all the time."

"What do you have in mind?"

"Well, it's just an idea, but if we created a new corporation to oversee both schools, perhaps we could complement each other. I can run the business side, and you can go back to being a visionary and an activist. I think my board would go for it if you agree."

Paul stabbed at the lemon in his iced tea with a straw. "So what do you want to tell your board tonight?"

"Only that you and I talked and, if you agree, that you're open to exploring the possibilities."

Paul thought about what Rafe had told him, how ignorance breeds fear and fear creates enemies. "Tell your board that I'm not only open to exploring the possibilities, I'm excited about it."

17

A Lucky Coin Is
What You Make of It

PAUL WATCHED PHYLLIS WALK DOWN THE STREET AND WONdered at the fact that after all these years of competing with each other, she had called today. Her board-meeting crisis and his bank-meeting crisis had brought them together. Who knows? Perhaps she'd had a visit from Rafe as well. Paul recalled one of Buddha's sayings: *To be awake is to be amazed all the time.*

It was only one thirty, so Paul took the long way around to the lot where he'd parked. As he walked along Main Street, the feeling of déjà vu that had pervaded his whole day became almost overwhelming. It climaxed when he looked down a dark alleyway. Just past a big blue garbage Dumpster a man was stretched out on the ground under a makeshift blanket of newspapers. Paul's head spun with the odor of garbage; there was no mistaking that he'd been here before. The alcoholic was sound asleep, empty bottle not far from his head, just as it had been in the dream. Paul watched the wall for a moment; when no picture appeared, he knelt and softly stroked the man's cheek. He knew that if he walked on down the alley, he'd see an old man and a little boy waiting at the bus stop; he also knew there was no need to go look.

Back out on Main Street Paul stopped at a newsstand for a chocolate bar. It was one forty-five. He stepped into a phone booth and dialed. "Mr. Weatherford's office, please. . . . Hi, this is Paul Peterson. Would you please let Marty know that I'll be about fifteen minutes late. Apologize for me, but I've been unavoidably detained. Thanks. Oh, sorry, one more thing. Could you check some account balances for me?"

Paul read his account numbers into the receiver and waited for a moment. Then he smiled and instructed that money be transferred into his two mortgage accounts and a receipt be given to Mr. Weatherford prior to their meeting.

The whole time he talked on the phone, his eyes never left the entrance to the alley. In his dream they had been running late for the bank meeting. He recalled the dashboard clock reading one fifty-six when Rafe stopped time for their alleyway sojourn. Paul unwrapped his chocolate bar and leaned against a lamppost. It was one fifty-one. A police car coming down Main Street slowed at the alley's entrance, then accelerated past. Paul took a bite of chocolate.

He never saw the car. Not really. The image just sort of hung there in the back of his eyes, like the psychedelic fantasies that float by in the aftermath of a camera flash. Frozen car, frozen driver, two lines of frozen motion in the alleyway, then nothing. Gone. Just a fading flash at the

WHETHER SOMETHING IS A
RANDOM COINCIDENCE OR A
MEANINGFUL CONNECTION
DEPENDS UPON HOW YOU
CHOOSE TO INTERPRET IT.

back of the retinas. Or a figment of the frontal lobes. No telling which. Had he been watching himself watching himself? Or buzzing out on chocolate? No telling.

One thing Paul had grown to believe during his ten years of working with Shay's Point School was this: There is no such thing as a coincidence. Things always happen for a reason. Too many times the phone had rung at just the right moment, the caller offering just what he needed to keep it all together, for him to write it off to blind luck. It is only blind if you aren't looking for the connections.

Serendipity. The knack for making neat discoveries without planning to. *I might not be able to manage a shoeshine stand*, Paul thought, *but I've got serendipity.* He smiled at the thought, but it was true. He trusted his luck. And the more he trusted his luck, the less he had to rely upon it. No matter what happened, things would always work out for the best. What was it Rafe had said—with faith fear becomes an ally.

Paul stopped at his car door. There on the ground at his feet was a coin. He leaned over and picked up a silver dollar.

What sign might a guardian angel leave to signify that you're on the right track? What if it were a guardian angel who knew that the main thing preventing you from achieving some important goal was the fear of running out of money?

Rafe had been there.

18

Take Your Purpose Seriously

It was already two fifteen when Paul wheeled into the bank's parking ramp. There was a line of cars in front of him, inching its way forward like a caterpillar on a tree, stopping to explore every fresh opening. Fifteen minutes later Paul had reached the top and was coming back down. Then a space beckoned him, big and wide—right there by the door. He pulled in over the wheelchair painted on the asphalt. It was almost half an hour later than it had been in the dream—maybe the parking enforcers had already made their rounds and he would escape the ticket.

Paul punched the button for the elevator then, knowing it would be full, decided not to wait and ran down the stairs. He pushed open the door and found himself in the back alley as the door closed behind him with an authoritative snap. "Dammit, Rafe, dreams are supposed to be anatomically correct! What the hell am I doing in the alley?" A

man peered out from behind a Dumpster at the yelling, then darted back when Paul glared in his direction.

Paul was midalley. Either way he was going to have to walk halfway around the building to get to the front door. With a resigned sigh, he started walking. He couldn't avoid being late, but he could at least enjoy the walk.

"Hi. Paul Peterson, here to see Marty Weatherford."

"Yes, Mr. Peterson, he's expecting you. Come on back." Sarah—that's what the plaque on her desk named the lady guarding the door to the administration offices—rose and shook Paul's hand.

"You mean he's not in the big conference room?"

"Excuse me?"

"Um, never mind. I just thought with all the lawyers and everything we'd need a bigger room."

"As far as I know, Mr. Peterson, you're the only lawyer who's going to be here."

Marty Weatherford came out from his office to greet them in the hall. He squashed Paul's hand and dragged him toward his office. "Hey, buddy, it's been too long. We've got to get out on the courts again soon. If you get too rusty, I might even be able to beat you."

Paul laughed as he sat in one of Marty's leather armchairs. Marty played racquetball the way he had wrestled in college, where he ranked nationally. Paul was lucky to get a few points per game.

"Thanks for sending me the receipt on those mortgage balances. I tell you what, the loan committee meets on Friday and I was sweating what to tell them about my friend who only gets around to making his mortgage payments every three months or so." Marty laughed again, but even

IF YOU DON'T TAKE YOUR
PURPOSE SERIOUSLY, HOW CAN
YOU EXPECT THAT
ANYONE ELSE WILL?

more than when they were on the racquetball court, Paul
sensed how intimidating it must have been to face Marty
on the wrestling mat.

"Listen to me, Paul." Marty was no longer smiling. "I've
got to talk to you now, not as your friend or your racquetball partner but as your banker. You know, you just
can't run that school like some kid's lemonade stand anymore. I've never seen an audit report come back with so
many management recommendations. You're just asking
for trouble, running things so higgledy-piggledy like that.
For cryin' out loud, you don't even have your finances on a
computer, man. Did you, like, miss the turnoff for the
1990s or something?"

Paul felt Rafe's silver dollar through his pocket. What
was the lesson here? Where was the connection? "I never
made any money on lemonade stands when I was a kid, and
I guess on that score not much has changed. Maybe I'm
missing a gene or something."

"Well, you'd better find it pretty quick. Or find some
other way to compensate for it." Marty still wasn't smiling.
Paul felt the fear of a weaker opponent being stalked by a
champion. "Paul, what you're doing is important. Really
important. Too important to let fail because you're not
willing to manage it.

"Most people in this world just have jobs, Paul. Look at
me. I come in here every day and loan people money, and
when they don't pay it back, I break their kneecaps." Marty
smiled and Paul smiled, but they both knew he wasn't trying to be funny. "But you've got a calling. And with a
calling comes an extra responsibility to take it seriously.

"My sister's kid got mixed up in drugs. Got kicked out of

school. They came home one day and found him shot dead. Nice kid, not much older than your Jeffie. Shot dead! You're doing a good thing at that school, a noble thing. But if you're going to do it, Paul, please do it right. You won't help anyone if you go under."

Paul regarded his racquetball nemesis. There was a tender spot under that wrought-iron exterior, which he'd never seen before. "What do you suggest, Marty?"

"You can't do it all on your own, man. Get some help." Marty pulled a business card out of his shirt pocket and handed it to Paul. "Give Butch a call. He's a retired accountant, done a lot of work auditing nonprofit organizations like yours. Now he's just doing some volunteer work to keep busy. I took the liberty of speaking with him. He supports your cause and wants to help."

They made a date for a racquetball game, and Paul turned to leave. Catching Sarah's bemused stare out of the corner of his eye as he walked through the anteroom, he remarked, "He's really an alright guy when he's not surrounded by lawyers, isn't he?"

In the parking lot there was a seventy-five-dollar ticket under his windshield wiper. "Thanks for the silver dollar, Rafe. Now I just need seventy-four more."

Paul smiled as he stuck the ticket in his pocket. Nothing was going to ruin his day.

19

COMMITMENT IS THE FOUNDATION
OF PERSEVERANCE

IT HARDLY SEEMED LIKE A YEAR HAD PASSED SINCE PAUL'S CRISIS
with the bank, his meeting Rafe, and setting off on a whole
new direction with the school. Perhaps Rafe had been right
about the relativity of time—the train was certainly moving
faster these days.

Paul's Chevy crunched across the gravel parking lot,
then sputtered into silence after he turned off the ignition.
It was one year ago to the day that he had last walked up
the hill before him, one year ago that he had met Rafe.
Looking at the Chevy's odometer, which he had pushed
well into six figures with his travels over the past year, Paul
wondered if the old hulk would be up for another backward
race through time.

The door creaked open against Paul's shove and he
climbed out. His own creaking joints reminded him that he
was holding up hardly any better than the car. The park
was deserted, just as it had been a year ago. As he trudged

ESPECIALLY OVER THE LONG
TERM, YOU CAN DO MORE THAN
YOU THINK YOU CAN DO.
DON'T CHEAT YOURSELF BY
ACCEPTING ANEMIC GOALS.

up the hill, Paul could see that the impending sunset would, if anything, be more spectacular than the one into which he had jumped one year earlier.

It had not been just a dream, of that Paul was sure. At the crest of the hill he hesitated. He had long pondered where he would go first—straight ahead to the edge of the cliff, or off to the right toward the spot where he and Rafe had first spoken. Standing quietly with his hands clasped in front of him, Paul waited to see if he felt pulled in either direction. As the sun touched the western horizon, he walked to the edge of the cliff.

So much had happened since he last stood on this spot. They had gone ahead with the merger of his school and New Trails, and Paul had given up routine administrative responsibilities. Phyllis had helped to secure a large donation to be used for developing the philosophies and practices Paul had pioneered at Shay's Point into a package that could be implemented in other communities. For the past six months he had been traveling almost nonstop selling the concept and helping people start it up.

The Miracle of the Leap, as Paul and Joan now called his experience with Rafe, had not eliminated stress and anxiety from his life. Far from it—the demands of creating a national program were heavier than any he had ever known. He most regretted that his travel schedule kept him from spending as much time as he wanted with his family.

But he had learned to overcome the doubt that before the Miracle of the Leap made his life so miserable. Now when he did have time with his family, he never felt guilty for not being at work. Having more clearly defined his personal mission helped him avoid spending time on things that weren't really important. And his new vision, in which someday troubled kids everywhere would have a place to go and someone to be on their side, crowded out the nagging voices that reminded him of everything else he wasn't doing.

He had given himself permission to dream a big dream and then to work hard to make it come true. Along the way he had been helped by many new and unexpected friends. Although his frequent travel took him from his family more than he wished, the quest in which they all believed had also brought them closer together.

Paul took a step closer to the edge and looked down. The sea was more turbulent than it had been a year ago, and the waves crashed over the rock upon which he had been broken. A part of him was still down there—the part that had once thought he could make it on his own. The part, he smiled to think, that had once looked down its long, arrogant nose at people who, he believed, had money but no meaning.

The sun was halfway set, sending a perfectly symmetrical spray of silver needles into a crimson sky. Paul wanted to step back away from the edge, but was rooted in place, mesmerized by an inner voice daring him to fall forward, to put Rafe to the test. *It's a beautiful evening for flying*, it mocked, and a part of Paul longed for the exhilaration of free fall into a web of faith.

Defying the voice, Paul made an uneventful trip to Rafe's meeting place. From there he watched the sun take its final bow, knowing that he would never again see it rise from that spot. Above, in just the place it had been a year ago, the prick of light that he called Rafestar began to emerge, and Paul's thoughts went out to Jack O'Mara.

One of the first things he did after the Miracle of the Leap was to hire Jack as a custodian for the school. But with Paul's consent, six months later Phyllis fired him for coming to school drunk for the third time. Jack was not yet ready for his miracle.

Paul pulled a battered index card from his shirt pocket. It held the notes he made right after his day with Rafe:

Caring is the root of courage.

Courage is the fuel of commitment.

Commitment is the foundation of perseverance.

Perseverance is the agent of change.

Tonight Paul would be giving a speech at the first national meeting of New Trails School Systems. Phyllis, he thought with a smile, had even come up with a better name than he had, which they agreed to use for the new corporation. Paul was going to talk about Rafe, and about the Miracle of the Leap.

The podium stood under a huge banner that read:

NEVER FEAR, NEVER QUIT

As Paul heard himself being introduced and looked out at the expectant audience, he momentarily wished that Rafe would appear and rescue him from having to go on stage.

Public speaking petrified him; the largest audience he had heretofore addressed fit comfortably in the Shay's Point auditorium. Joan gave him an encouraging squeeze; Rafe would not save him now.

Conquering fear was getting easier all the time. Paul looked this particular fear in the face, named it "the universal worry that your pants will fall down right up there in front of all those people," and stepped up to the podium.

"Those of you who know me well know that since I was a young man—which right now feels like it was a very long time ago—there has been a spot that holds a special place in my heart. From Shay's Point you can see a sunset like you'll never see anywhere else. But not many people go there, because the road is long and rocky, and out on the point it's usually cold and windy. When Joan and I started the school, though, there was no question we would call it Shay's Point.

"A little over a year ago I went up to Shay's Point planning to jump off the edge. I had been so blinded by my own worries and insecurities that it seemed there was no way out except down. I hope, my friends, that you will not think less of me for it, but jumping off the cliff onto the rocks below Shay's Point that evening saved me."

There was an awful stillness in the room, as if Paul had just announced that he had a dread disease and everyone was wondering whether they had gotten close enough to catch it.

Never Fear, Never Quit. Paul gathered up his courage to continue.

He told the whole story. Unedited and unadulterated. How he had been defeated by his own fear and yet, from

THE MOST BEAUTIFUL MIRACLE
OCCURS WHEN SOMEONE IS
ABLE TO MAKE CHANGES IN
HIMSELF THAT HE BELIEVED
WOULD HAVE BEEN IMPOSSIBLE.
PROFOUND SELF-
TRANSFORMATION IS A GIFT OF
GRACE THAT IS AVAILABLE TO US
ALL. BUT IT COMES WITH A
PRICE TAG; IT MUST BE REPAID
THROUGH SERVICE AND
SHARING.

the wreckage of failure, was rescued by a power far beyond his understanding, much less his control. Why he no longer felt so certain about the nature of "reality," and how in any event reality did not really seem so real anymore, now that he knew how malleable it was in the hands of a master like Rafe. And that being broken on the rocks below Shay's Point allowed him to be rebuilt in a stronger and more functional shape, although with fewer fragile adornments.

As he spoke, the appalled silence softened. Understanding nods here and there throughout the audience told him that he was not the only one who had experienced Rafe's intervention.

How big my family has become now that I do not judge people through the distorting lens of my own fears.

As the audience rose in applause, Paul waved Joan up to the stage to join him. In the back of the room he saw The One he had not seen in a year smile and nod, then turn and walk out through the closed door.

20

MIRACLES ARE MADE TO BE SHARED

PAUL PETERSON FELT NO SADNESS AS HE LOOKED DOWN UPON the ceremony. It was a beautiful June day, bedecked with butterflies and serenaded by birds. Off in the distance the cries of happy children vivified the circle of life. A soft breeze blew in from the ocean, drifted over Shay's Point, and rustled new leaves on the cemetery's old oak trees.

Joan looked so diminutive, standing there between Jeff and Sandra, leaning against her walking cane, but to Paul she had never appeared more beautiful. He now knew what she could only believe: that the two of them had always been together, would always be together, and that she, too, would soon transcend the confines of earthly time and that they would soar together above the tracks, seeing past, future, sunshine, and tunnels all at once.

Jeff stood tall and grim, so much like his father had been at midlife. Not so long ago Paul had stood between Jeff and Joan for the funeral of Jeff's youngest son. Jeff's faith was

WHATEVER YOU MOST NEED IN

LIFE, THE BEST WAY FOR YOU TO

GET IT IS TO HELP SOMEONE

ELSE GET IT WHO NEEDS IT

EVEN MORE THAN YOU DO.

now being challenged in a way Paul's never was. Paul had learned much, but did not yet understand why he would be reunited with Jonathan before the boy's father was.

To Joan's right stood Sandra, at once a grown woman with a family of her own and the gap-toothed imp who had given Paul "merpission" to dream new dreams. Now a successful writer, Sandra had always given herself permission to follow her own path, and had never flinched nor faltered during her times of doubt and adversity.

Paul had occasionally wondered what would be said about him at his funeral, and in fact had often asked his students to write their own obituaries as part of a goal-setting exercise. Now, though, the words held no interest for him and were lost to the breeze.

The wind picked up, causing the images below to gradually lose their separate identity and meld together. Paul simultaneously felt himself merging into the scene below and being pulled upward.

"It's a beautiful evening for flying, isn't it?"

Rafe looked exactly as he had on that day nearly fifty years ago when he had plucked Paul from the air below Shay's Point. Paul wondered whether he, too, appeared as he had that day, or as a newborn infant, or as an old man. Whatever it was, he knew, was an illusion soon to change.

"You'll see everyone again, my dear old friend, but it's time now for you and me to move on." The funeral faded away as Paul and his old friend flew off toward the distant mountains, at last landing on an eyrie that seemed to overlook this half of the universe.

Paul felt no need to talk in the presence of his friend as they sat together looking out across the world. Finally Rafe spoke. In his lap he held a simple unadorned box. "You've done well, Paul; you've written a lovely story, one that will be read for a long time to come."

Paul shook his head. "I didn't write any stories, Rafe, though I may have told a tale or two. Sandra is the writer of the family."

Rafe smiled and opened the box. Inside, Paul could see a book in a soft leather cover. Rafe cradled his hands under it, as though he were lifting a baby eagle out of its nest. As Rafe extended the book toward him, Paul read the words inscribed on the front:

> THE PRINCIPLES OF
> COURAGE AND PERSEVERANCE
> by Paul Peterson

As he caressed the cover, a thousand memories raced through Paul's mind; the same compression of reality he had experienced in the fall from Shay's Point, but without the terror. He gently lifted the cover and read the first heading:

Caring Is the Root of Courage

Though Paul did not remember having written the lessons, they were clearly part of his story; over a lifetime they were the principles he had learned and had taught to many.

"You are not finished with your teaching, my friend."

"I hope not, Rafe. It would be unfortunate if everyone had to learn these lessons from scratch."

Rafe laughed with the deep, rich tenor that had once led Paul to expect to see Moses. "Paul, the universe is very efficient. Nothing is ever wasted, especially not the lessons of life. It's been said on earth that when the student is ready to learn, a teacher appears. And I believe that your first student is nearly ready. So we had better hurry up and teach you to fly on your own—at least better than you did at Shay's Point."

Paul felt the weight of the book suddenly leave his hands and, looking down, saw that there were no hands there at all.

"It's really quite easy, Paul. Stretch your wings, lean forward into the wind, and give a little push with your legs."

Paul tried to respond, but could only make a shrill squawking noise.

"Don't worry. Your voice will come back to you when you need it again. Now, follow me."

Paul was amazed at how precisely he could see the finest details of the eagle perched beside him, and at how clearly every distant tree and stone appeared on the periphery of his vision.

Rafe squawked at Paul, spread his wings, and pushed off into the wind. As he watched his old friend silhouetted against the setting sun, Paul realized that he would not need lessons to learn to fly.

Paul Peterson spread his new wings and leaned forward into the sunset.

The eagle soared down from the North Rim along Bright Angel Creek. Paul had never seen the Grand Canyon so fresh and green. Gliding up and down the Canyon walls, from the dark metamorphic stone near the river to the sandstones and limestones higher up the towering cliffs, he could see the unfolding of over a billion years of the earth's history.

At the junction of Bright Angel Creek and the Colorado River, he wheeled to the east and soared out over the Tonto Plateau, freshly watered blackbrush giving it the hue of a green chalkboard. Catching an updraft, he rocketed up and over Zoroaster's Temple, in his mind the most sacred of all the Canyon's rock cathedrals, and then spiraled down around its flanks, chasing off a pair of ravens. Playing out the wind, he kited eastward along the river all the way to Marble Canyon, then wheeled back around, flying into the setting sun.

No human had ever seen the Canyon this way, and none ever would. Paul longed to stay a little longer, to watch the sun's setting transform the Canyon into a living sculpture. But his sharp eyes saw the gray pickup truck pull into the parking lot at Mather Point and come to a stop fifty feet short of the guardrail.

Paul raced the wind as the sun approached the horizon. Although he was still nearly a mile from the point, he saw white smoke belching out of the truck's tailpipes and, inside, the driver's arm moving as he put it into gear.

At the moment the sun kissed the earth, the truck's tires started to spin, blowing off a gale of white smoke. They caught with a shriek, and the truck lurched forward. As it smashed through the railing and hung suspended, Paul saw the look on the driver's face through the side window, grim and determined. In the seat next to him, invisible to human eyes but now, finally, evident to Paul, was the ghost of fear, every bit as hideous as he'd ever imagined.

The pickup quickly lost its forward momentum and the hood turned downward. It fell free for several seconds before the front bumper caught on a rock outcropping, yanking the headlights in toward the Canyon wall and flipping the truck bed outward. The somersault slammed the roof into the rock wall, crushing it flat; on the second roll the bed broke away from the cab, rupturing the fuel tanks. Though it seemed to Paul that the sparks floated in the air forever before igniting the gasoline, he knew it was only microseconds.

The flaming wreckage avalanched its way past hundreds of millions of years of rock creation before landing in a pyre of metal and rubber far below the dangling guardrail of Mather Point.

Even at his altitude high above the point, Paul could feel the updrafts being created by the inferno four thousand feet and 500 million years below. He spiraled around the black plume that was building from below as he waited for the miracle to begin.

It wasn't obvious when time reversed its course. He'd expected to feel some sort of wrenching sensation, like when he'd rejoined his own physical body after the leap off Shay's Point. But the first indication was the sight of people running backward away from the guardrail. The black smoke stopped its upward drift and slowly started to work its way back down toward the truck.

Paul swooped up over the parking lot, not having any

desire to get closer to the truck in its present condition, and landed in a pine tree. Presently he heard a horrible grinding noise coming closer and closer, and then the tail end of the pickup exploded back through the guardrail, pulling the splintered pieces back into place as it came, engine gunning and tires squealing.

Then it was totally silent.

The sun was barely above the horizon, and frozen in place. Paul gingerly climbed out of the tree, glad that in solidified time no one saw the clumsiness of the human body that felt so burdensome compared with the efficient feathered frame waiting for him in the tree.

John Parker was standing near the guardrail, about fifty feet from where his truck would soon go barreling by. His hair blowing in the wind was the only movement on the frozen landscape; his image sat behind the wheel of the truck, unaware of the ghost of fear at his side.

Paul felt the light breeze coming from the west, opposite its direction when time was moving forward. Rafe had promised him that his voice would come back when he needed it. Never fear, never quit. Paul placed his hand on John Parker's shoulder.

"It's a beautiful evening for flying, isn't it?"

Acknowledgments

A NUMBER OF YEARS AGO, I LOST A JOB. NOT REALLY A VERY BIG deal in the overall scheme of things; I was one of over three million Americans who lost jobs that year. Not one of us had to brave Sniper Alley in Sarejevo, face starvation in Somalia, or stand in front of tanks in Beijing. Still, for me, as for many, it was emotionally devastating. In retrospect, however, it was the source of an important learning and growing experience. I met my own Rafe, many times and in many guises.

My family has been a source of tremendous support: my parents, Joe and Janelle, who have supported me in everything; Sally, Annie, and Doug, who have cheerfully shared in new dreams that give us more freedom but fewer things; and Steven, Allen, and Nancy, who prove that brotherly and sisterly love outlasts sibling combat. Martha Ellen and Nellie are the world's greatest great-grandmothers.

Special friends gave me moral support and an occasional

sanctuary for thinking and writing, including Al and Ellen Cram, Jeff and Sandra Rinz, Bill Townsley, and Kathleen Townsley. Anyone suffering emotional dislocation should enjoy the friendship of spiritual ministers like Doug Peters, Bill Chidester, and Mike Crosby, and counselors like Bob King and Jay Cooper.

Special thanks to Thom Greenlaw, Brad Bevers, John Staley, Brandt Echternacht, and Doug Wakefield for giving me opportunities to try on new uniforms, and to the critical-care leadership team of the University of Iowa Hospitals and Clinics, who listened patiently to my awkward first few seminars. Everyone who has ever lost a job and then started a business needs the guidance of an attorney like Phil Leff, accountants like Verne Nelson and Al Meyer, and a bank like Hills Bank, which Dwight Seegmiller, Tom Cilek, and their dynamite staff have transformed into one of America's finest community banks. Greg Rufe, Mary Fuller, John Colloton, Sally Mathis, Steve Ummel, Dick Pettingill, Cliff Eldredge, Mike Daly, Dan Rissing, and Mike Kieffer have been great career mentors.

Outward Bound helped me find my spirit in the desert, the Iowa City Zen Center helped me find my soul on a zafu, and the University of Iowa Writers Workshop helped me find my voice on a yellow pad. Millard and Linda Fuller, founders of Habitat for Humanity, are supreme role models. Many writers and philosophers helped me stop searching for answers and start searching for questions. I especially appreciate the irreverent poetry of McZen, who taught me that God has a loving sense of humor.

Thanks to the thousands of volunteers, donors, and

workers in the movement to stop the tobacco industry from using glamorous, sophisticated, and fraudulent marketing to push a lethal, addictive drug. There is a huge smoke-free room in my heart for all the friends I've made working with STAT. I wish I could mention everyone.

John Slade was member number one in 1985 and became president in 1995. Dave Altman helped me organize our first community projects ten years ago and has become one of my dearest friends. Henry and Edith Everett have been unfaltering in their support. Jodi Teel was one of our earliest supporters. Ann, Barb, Denise, Diane, Gail, and Laura are the greatest staff possible.

Dr. C. Everett Koop has been more than a hero and an inspiration; whenever we've asked for help only he could provide, he's made space on a calendar that needs more time, not more work. As then-president of the Henry J. Kaiser Family Foundation, Dr. Al Tarlov supported our infant organization. Robert Wood Johnson Foundation president Dr. Steve Schroeder and senior program officer Mike Beachler helped the organization move into maturity.

At various difficult times in my life, people have helped me in the way that Rafe helped Paul Peterson. The memories of Mark Mathis, Ann Moore, and Dr. John Gibbs continue to be a source of strength and courage for me and for many others.

Since the first edition of *Never Fear, Never Quit* was published, it's become the foundation for a growing national movement of *self-empowerment through faith and action*. I am grateful to everyone who has helped us build momentum behind the Never Fear, Never Quit Ultimate Success Conferences. The first one was made possible through the unstinting support of our sponsors, including the chambers of commerce in Iowa City and Cedar Rapids, *The Gazette* of Cedar Rapids, Iowa Book and Supply, the *National Business Employment Weekly*, American Express Financial Advisors, the North Dodge Athletic Club, PIP Printing, Active Endeavors, and the Professional Women's Network. The conference was made a terrific success by our speakers, including Mark Victor Hansen, Laurie Beth Jones, Thomas J. Winninger, Dottie Walters, Tony Lee, and all of the *National Business Employment Weekly* authors, Angie Lee, Art Mortell, Hunter Fulghum, David Miln Smith, and Deborah Scaling Kiley. The conference would never have happened without the hard work of people in the Never Fear, Never Quit office, including Chris Kasik, Denise Prull, Leslie Lehman, Tony Holets, and Sally, Annie, and Doug Tye.

I especially appreciate the advice and support of my literary agent Faith Hamlin at the Sanford Greenburger Agency; Stephanie Gunning, senior editor at Dell Publishing; Arlynn Greenbaum at the Authors Unlimited speakers bureau; and Dottie Walters of the Walters International Speakers Bureau.

Shortly after I finished this book, I was studying the principles of success and self-empowerment. While sitting alone in a room lit by a single candle, it struck me that the most pervasive theme in all of this wisdom is that real success and happiness *requires* spiritual faith in the transcendent meaning of life and submission to the will of a higher power. At that very moment a loving presence, every bit as real to me as Rafe was to Paul Peterson, touched me and said softly, "Joe, you finally figured it out." Not even alone in the wilderness have I felt so close to God, to whom I am an inadequate and disobedient, but increasingly grateful, charge.

Never Fear, Never Quit is a fast-growing international movement that promotes self-empowerment through faith and action. For a free copy of *Never Fear, Never Quit News*, the quarterly newspaper that is packed with ideas, strategies, and inspirations for living and working with courage and perseverance, please contact us at:

Never Fear, Never Quit
P.O. Box 480
Solon, IA 52333-0480

Phone   319-644-3889
Fax   319-644-3963
E-mail nfnq@aol.com

Joe Tye is a frequent speaker on personal success and organizational effectiveness. He can be reached at the above address.

THE NEVER FEAR, NEVER QUIT™ PLEDGE

With faith, fear becomes an ally and adversity becomes a teacher.

* I will take full responsibility for my own happiness, for my own success, and for my own life.

* I will not blame other people for my problems, nor will I allow low self-esteem, self-limiting beliefs, or the negativity of others to talk me out of achieving what I am capable of achieving and becoming the person I am capable of being.

* I will have faith that, though I may not understand why adversity happens, by my conscious choice I can find strength, compassion, and grace through my trials.

* I will face rejection and failure with courage, awareness, and perseverance, making these experiences the platform for future acceptance and success.

* I will do the things I'm afraid to do, but which I know should be done. Sometimes this will mean asking for help to do that which I can't do by myself.

* I will earn the help I need in advance by helping other people now, and repay the help I receive by serving others later.

* When I fall down, I will get back up, whatever it takes.

* My faith in God and my gratitude for all that I have been blessed with will shine through in my attitudes and in my actions.